Mood Disorders:
An Introduction

Caleb W. Lack

Mood Disorders: An Introduction
Copyright © 2013 Caleb W. Lack

Published by *Onus Books*

Printed by Lightning Source International

Cover design: Onus Books

Trade paperback ISBN: 978-0-9566948-8-1

OB 03/07

10 9 8 7 6 5 4 3 2 1

About the author:

Caleb W. Lack, Ph.D. is an Assistant Professor of Psychology and Counseling Practicum Coordinator in the Department of Psychology at the University of Central Oklahoma.

A clinical psychologist licensed to practice in both Oklahoma and Arkansas, Dr. Lack is the author of more than three dozen scientific publications relating to the assessment and treatment of psychological problems such as Obsessive-Compulsive Disorder, Tourette's Syndrome, pediatric mood disorders, and posttraumatic stress. In addition, Dr. Lack has presented nationwide and internationally at conferences on a variety of topics, including children's reactions to natural disasters, computer-based treatment of substance abuse, innovative teaching and training methods, and more. He is on the editorial board of several scientific journals and a reviewer for both journals and granting agencies.

Dr. Lack's clinical interest in evidence-based practice developed while in graduate school for Clinical Psychology at Oklahoma State University and during his predoctoral internship in Clinical Child/Pediatric Psychology at the University of Florida. He specializes in the treatment of children and adults with anxiety disorders (particularly obsessive-compulsive disorder), psychological assessment, and has extensive experience with persons with chronic tics and Tourette's Syndrome. He has consulted for and been interviewed by local, national, and international media outlets.

In addition to courses on his clinical and research specialties in the anxiety disorders and evidence-based psychological practice, Dr. Lack also teaches undergraduate and graduate courses on critical thinking, science, and pseudoscience. These recently culminated in the edited text *Science, Pseudoscience, & Critical Thinking* as well as a series of documentaries on pseudoscience and superstition in Oklahoma. He writes the "Great Plains Skeptic" column on the Skeptic Ink Network, as well as presenting about skepticism and critical thinking frequently.

A native Oklahoman, Dr. Lack grew up in the rural community of Mountain View, where his parents still reside and farm and ranch on land that has been owned by the family for close to 100 years. He currently resides in Edmond, Oklahoma with his beautiful wife and brilliant son on a wonderful little property called Freethought Farm.

Learn more about Dr. Lack at www.caleblack.com

This book is dedicated to the innumerable researchers and clinicians who made possible the evidence-based treatments described in this book. Their remarkable accomplishments have led to the direct improvement of millions of lives.

CONTENTS

What is a Mental Disorder?

The terms "mental disorder," "mental illness," and "psychopathology" are often used interchangeably by those in psychology and related fields; all refer to the study of unusual or abnormal behaviors that impair one's daily functioning. Unlike terms and concepts in many of the physical sciences, however, there is not a single, agreed-upon by all operational definition for these terms. The primary definitional conflict hinges on this question: Can mental disorders be defined as a scientific term, or are they instead socially constructed?

This lack of a single definition can lead to confusion and communication problems both when mental health professionals, such as psychologists, psychiatrists, counselors, or social workers, attempt to talk to each other and to the general public. As a result, mental disorders are used and defined in a variety of ways. Before beginning our examination of anxiety disorders, we must discuss these definitions and decide which one (or ones) will guide this book. Below are descriptions of the most common perspectives.

Mental Disorders as Statistical Deviance

The statistical deviance perspective has enormous common sense appeal, as it involves defining abnormal behavior by comparing an individual's behavior to the frequency of occurrence of the same behavior in the general population. A behavior is considered abnormal if it occurs rarely or infrequently in the general population. This definition lends itself very well to measurement, as researchers and clinicians can administer objective assessments to clients and get accurate measurements of just how far their depression, anxiety, hyperactivity, and so on are from the norm. As such, this definition is often seen as highly scientific.

Unfortunately, several problems are apparent when this model is examined closely. First, who determines how far from the norm is too far from the norm? It is not as if there is a stone tablet handed down from the psychopathology gods that has "Behaviors that are two or more standard deviations from the norm shall be considered abnormal" written on it. Instead, researchers and clinicians make that decision. Often, behaviors are considered "abnormal" if they occur in less than 5% of the population (1.645 standard deviations from the mean), but this is an entirely arbitrary cutoff. Another concern is that the tests that measure one's deviation are developed from within a particular cultural framework. In other words, there is not an objective, scientific definition of "obsessive-compulsive disorder," there is only the definition that the researchers developing the measure have (and someone else may not agree with it).

It is also worth noting that when viewing behavior, both sides of the normal curve would be considered "abnormal." So, according to this model, both someone with very high and very low general anxiety would be considered abnormal. In the real world, though, it is usually only one tail of the curve that is viewed as problematic or abnormal. For illustrative purposes, picture someone with an IQ of 70 and another person with an IQ of 130. On a scale where 100 is the average, with a standard deviation of 15, both are equally deviant from "normal" intelligence. Most people, however, would only consider the person with extremely low IQ to have a mental disorder, another problem with this conception.

Mental Disorders as Social Deviance

In the social deviance perspective, behavior is deemed abnormal if it deviates greatly from the accepted social standards, values, and norms of an individual's culture. This is different from the statistical perspective described above, as this method is uninterested in the *actual* norms of the population. This is because a population may have accepted standards that the majority of the culture do not actually meet. An example of this would be using alcohol and tobacco prior to the legal age of use, which would be considered unlawful and socially unacceptable, yet major surveys show that over 75% of high school seniors have consumed alcohol.

The problems with the social norms perspective are fairly obvious. First, there is little to no objective validity, due to individuals and groups even within the same culture having different ideas of what is socially acceptable. Second, what is acceptable at one point in time can become unacceptable with the passage of time, or vice versa. Until 1973, for example, homosexuality was classified as a diagnosable mental disorder by the American Psychiatric Association, rather than being recognized as a normal variation of sexual orientation. Finally, the different morals and standards of disparate cultural groups would mean that what was normal in one country or region would be considered abnormal in another.

Mental Disorders as Maladaptive Behavior

The maladaptive behavior perspective attempts to classify as mental disorders those behaviors that are dysfunctional. This refers to the effectiveness or ineffectiveness of a behavior in dealing with challenges or accomplishing goals. Typically discussed maladaptive behaviors include physically harmful behaviors, behaviors that prevent the person from taking care of themselves, those that prevent communication with others, and those that interfere with social bonding and relationships. As with our other perspectives, there are major concerns with this one.

First, how adaptive a behavior is hard to objectively quantify. This is due to the fact that the adaptive level of any particular behavior is based on both the situation and one's subjective judgment. If a person is engaging in coercive behaviors, stealing, and lying to others, most people would say those are maladaptive behaviors (and depending on his age, qualify you for a diagnosis of Conduct Disorder or Antisocial Personality Disorder). But what if you learn that he was doing this to obtain food or medicine for his family? Would that still be maladaptive? One's culture also plays a large role in determining the adaptiveness of a behavior. For instance, in many Native American tribes, it is considered disrespectful to look an elder directly in the eye when talking to them. In other cultures, though, it would be considered disrespectful to *not* look them in the eye. Finally, this perspective clashes mightily with the statistical deviance perspective, in that statistically deviant behaviors (e.g., an IQ higher than 99% of the population) can be highly adaptive, and that numerous maladaptive behaviors (such as fear of public speaking) are quite common in the population as a whole.

Dimensional vs. Categorical Models of Mental Disorders

Another, different way to think about mental disorders is captured in the concept of categories versus dimensions. In a categorical model, psychopathology is dichotomous, either being present or not being present. In other words, you either have a mental disorder, or you don't, there is no in-between. Dimensional models, on the other hand, acknowledge the fact that the vast majority of human behavior exists on a continuum, rather than the polarized view of the categorical model. What tends to be labeled as abnormal and unusual are merely the far ends of this normal curve of behavior. In this model, then, mental disorders are just extreme variations of normal psychological phenomena or problems that many or most of us experience.

The dimensional model has a very large amount of scientific support, particularly in the area of personality disorders. Support has been found for dimensional models of many other disorders, though, including anxiety, depressive episodes, and even psychotic disorders. Unfortunately, however, the real-world often requires *caseness* or *non-*

caseness. In many instances one must be diagnosed with a particular mental disorder to obtain certain things, such as insurance reimbursement, special services at school, or disability benefits. This, subsequently, creates a tension between the need for categories and the lack of scientific support for them.

DSM Definitions of Mental Disorder

The Diagnostic and Statistical Manual of Mental Disorders (DSM) is published by the American Psychiatric Association, and is the most widely used classification system of mental disorders in the United States (outside of the U.S., both the DSM and the International Classifications of Disease, or ICD, are used). It provides diagnostic criteria for almost 300 mental disorders. But how exactly does it define mental disorder? In the most recent edition, published in 1994, the following features are considered descriptive of a mental disorder:

a) A clinically significant behavioral or psychological syndrome or pattern that occurs in an individual

b) Is associated with present distress (e.g., a painful symptom) or disability (i.e., impairment in one or more important areas of functioning) or with a significantly increased risk of suffering death, pain, disability, or an important loss of freedom

c) Must not be merely an expectable and culturally sanctioned response to a particular event, for example, the death of a loved one

d) A manifestation of a behavioral, psychological, or biological dysfunction in the individual

e) Neither deviant behavior (e.g., political, religious, or sexual) nor conflicts that are primarily between the individual and society are mental disorders unless the deviance or conflict is a symptom of a dysfunction in the individual

The DSM-IV goes on to state, though, that "no definition adequately specifies precise boundaries for the concept of "mental disorder" and that "the concept of mental disorder (like many other concepts in medicine and science) lacks a consistent operational definition that covers all situations." Even with those caveats, this definition has considerable concerns: What exactly does "clinically significant" mean? How much distress is enough distress and who determines that? Who says what is or is not "culturally sanctioned"? And last, but perhaps most important, what defines a "behavioral or psychological syndrome or pattern"?

The categorical nature of the DSM-IV is also of concern, and the authors even state that they recognize the actual, dimensional nature of mental disorders, but due to the need for caseness (as described above) must operate in a categorical nature. This, in turn, contributes to the high amount of diagnostic overlap, or comorbidity, present in clinical populations. In one of the most well-conducted studies to examine this issue, Ronald Kessler and his research team (2005) found that 26.2% of Americans met criteria for a mental disorder; of these, 45% met criteria for two or more disorders.

These concerns and questions are certainly on the minds of many researchers and clinicians, and in fact a special group was assembled to rework the definition of a mental disorder for the upcoming revision of the DSM, the DSM-5, which is scheduled to be published in May 2013. The proposed revision, which was made available both online at DSM5.org and in an article by D.J. Stein and colleagues (2010), is as follows.

a) A behavioral or psychological syndrome or pattern that occurs in an individual

b) That reflects an underlying psychobiological dysfunction

c) The consequences of which are clinically significant distress (e.g., a painful symptom) or disability (i.e., impairment in one or more important areas of functioning)

d) Must not be merely an expectable response to common stressors and losses (for example, the loss of a loved one) or a culturally sanctioned response to a particular event (for example, trance states in religious rituals)

e) That is not primarily a result of social deviance or conflicts with society

As in the DSM-IV definition, there are other proposed caveats or considerations. A mental disorder should, by this definition, have diagnostic validity, clinical utility, and be differentiated from other, similar disorders. In addition, it is again acknowledged that there is no precise boundary between normality and mental disorders, and that the addition or deletion of a condition from the DSM should have substantial potential benefits which outweigh potential harms. While this proposed definition, and the revisions to many disorders that actually specify measures to determine severity and symptom level, are certainly an improvement over the DSM-IV (which was, in turn an improvement over earlier versions), there are still concerns over this definition. Specifically, will such severity indicators be used in real-world practice, and how will the introduction of such dimensionality impact treatment, reimbursement, and diagnostic practices? Will the improved diagnostic categories decrease the amount of overlap and comorbidity seen in mental health settings?

What to Do?

Given the problems with all of the preceding definitions of a mental disorder, one might begin to question the need for such a term or concept. After all, if it cannot be easily and accurately defined, what use is it? If the DSM categories are problematic, then why diagnose using them? The simple answer is "We use them because we need them."

Humans are natural categorizers, with a need to group and order things that we encounter. Our diagnostic typologies reflect this underlying need. It is much easier to understand and communicate to someone that a client is diagnosed with obsessive-compulsive disorder and generalized anxiety than to say something like "Their general anxiety level is at the 87th percentile, while they also have more obsessive, intrusive thoughts than 94% of the population and a subsequent rate of compulsive, anxiety reducing behaviors greater than all but 16% of their peers." In many cases, dimensional models of psychopathology, although perhaps more accurate, may simply be too confusing and/or complex to be useful in the real world.

Doing diagnostic work, and giving a patient a diagnosis based on presenting symptoms and lab findings, is an enormous part of all health professions. This is true even though dimensional models actually make more sense for almost all of what are called diseases (e.g., "Your blood pressure is higher than 95% of males your age, weight, and fitness level" rather than "You have high blood pressure.") Given clinical psychology's development and outgrowth from medicine, it makes sense that diagnosis would be part of our heritage. In many ways, it also establishes the credibility of psychiatry and clinical psychology by allowing these professions to stake out their "territory." Having something like the DSM essentially says "These problems and dysfunctions are the domain of psychiatry, so you other types of health providers back off." Losing diagnoses as part of the profession would mean that, in essence, we were losing our domain of health care. These reasons are, of course, in addition to the facts discussed previously about how real-life requires caseness or non-caseness in many occasions.

So, we as a profession and a society need definitions of mental disorders, and yet there does not appear to be a scientific consensus or definition on what a mental disorder actually is. So if there can be no truly scientific definition, what are we left with?

Mental Disorders as Social Constructions

Mental disorders, mental illness, and psychopathology are best understood as products of our history and culture, and should not try to be defined as some sort of universal, scientific construct. Mental disorders are, in a very real sense, invented. This does not, however, mean that they are not real. Instead, our conception of what is and is not normal behavior is influenced by everything from social and cultural forces, to politics and economics, to which professional groups have the most influence and clout at the time new definitions are being written. Mental disorders, then, are social constructs, a concept that is constructed by a particular group (in this case, the committee members of the DSM Work Groups, who are in turn influenced by researchers, clinicians, politicians, lay people, industry, religious beliefs, and more).

Accepting that mental disorders are a social construct, for some, implies that they are somehow fake or unimportant. Nothing, in fact, could be further from the truth. To put this in perspective, consider a number of other social constructs: love, beauty, race, poverty, wealth, physical disease. Each of those is constructed, and you will see different definitions of each when moving across time and between cultures. This does not rob any of them of their importance, or make any of them less real. The same is true of mental disorders.

As an example, consider a typical human and virulent, invasive colony of *E. coli*: When certain strains are ingested by humans, and begin proliferating, it can cause an enormous amount of disruption to the host, so we (humans) label it as a bad bacterium. However, this organism is doing only what it has adapted to do, and is thus fulfilling the evolutionary directive to multiply and spread its genetic material. We have decided *as a society* that this species is bad, and our

9

health is paramount over its health, and thus call it a disease and infection. This is social constructionism.

Conclusions

Mental disorders are hard to define, even by those who make it their life's work to study and treat them. Although there are certainly faults and flaws with the most widely used and social constructed definition, that of the DSM, the drawn boundary between normal and abnormal are essential to clinical psychology as a profession, persons with mental illness, and society as a whole.

Key References

American Psychiatric Association (2000). Diagnostic and Statistical Manual of Mental Disorders, Fourth Edition, Text Revision. Washington DC: Author.

American Psychiatric Association (2011). Definition of a mental disorder. Retrieved from http://www.dsm5.org/proposedrevisi on/Pages/proposedrevision.aspx?rid=465 on June 28, 2011.

Bergner, R. M. (1997). What is psychopathology? And so what? Clinical Psychology: Science and Practice, 4, 235-248.

Brown, P. (1995). Naming and framing: The social construction of diagnosis and illness. Journal of Health and Social Behavior, 35 (Extra Issue), 34-52.

Eisenberg, L. (1988). The social construction of mental illness. Psychological Medicine, 18, 1-9.

Maddux, J.E., Gosselin, J.T., & Winstead, B.A. (2005). Conceptions of psychopathology: A social constructionist perspective. In J.E. Maddox & B.A. Winstead (Eds.), Psychopathology: foundations for a contemporary understanding. Mahwah, NJ: Lawrence Erlbaum Associates.

Stein, D.J., Phillips, K.A., Bolton, D., Fulford, K.W.M., Sadler, J.Z., & Kendler, K.S. (2010). What is a mental/psychiatric disorder? From DSM - IV to DSM - V. Psychological Medicine, 40, 1759 - 1765.

Widiger, T. A. (1997). The construct of mental disorder. Clinical Psychology: Science and Practice, 4, 262-266.

Introduction to the Mood Disorders

All of us experience minor fluctuations in mood on a daily basis. Events around us and our cognitive interpretations of them cause us to become happy or sad, excited or bored, outgoing or withdrawn. Such changes are a normal part of the human experience, and those without such changing emotions and moods are often seen as cold and uncaring, stoic and unfeeling. But what happens with a person's moods swing too high or too low? When these swings begin to cause problems with adaptive functioning, both for the individual and others in their environment? At that point, someone may qualify for a diagnosis of a mood disorder.

The commonality that binds these disorders is an intense and prolonged disturbance in mood state. In particular, someone is most often experiencing unexpected and functionally impairing decreases or elevations in mood, accompanied by a heterogeneous presentation of other symptoms. For the vast majority of those with a mood disorder, this will be a decrease in mood, or a depressive state, although some will also experience increases, or manic states, or both at the same time. The pattern of these states, or episodes as they are known in the DSM-IV, helps the clinician to determine exactly which mood disorder a person is experiencing.

There are two broad categories of mood disorders in the DSM-IV: unipolar and bipolar. In unipolar disorders, only a decrease in mood state, or a depression, is seen. The two unipolar mood disorders are major depressive disorder and dysthymic disorder. In bipolar disorders, both decreased (depressive episode) and increased (manic episode) states occur, and can even occur at the same time (mixed episode). Bipolar I disorder, bipolar II disorder, and cyclothymic disorder all fall into this category.

It is important to differentiate between culturally expected mood changes and a mood disorder. For example, it is normal and expected that one would experience depressive symptoms and a drop in mood when confronted with a major loss, such as a relative or close friend dying. Grief and the grieving process are universal, evolutionarily adaptive functions. They can allow one to obtain needed comfort, resources, and social support during a very trying time. A second, relatively common cause of depressive symptoms would be the "baby blues," also known as postpartum depression. Large scale studies have found depression rates as high as 13% in females after giving birth, even controlling for previous history of mood disorders.

While both unipolar and bipolar disorders are seen cross-culturally and around the world, there is a much larger range of prevalence rates seen for depression and dysthymia. In fact, rates of bipolar and cyclothymic disorders are fairly universal, with around 2.4% of the population worldwide meeting criteria for a bipolar spectrum disorder at some point in their life. In sharp contrast, lifetime rates of major depressive disorder vary widely across the globe, ranging from the extremely low (Taiwan at 1.5%) to very high (U.S. at 17%, France at 16.4%, Lebanon at 19.0%).

Much like the treatment options for anxiety disorders, there are both effective, evidence-based pharmacological and psychological treatments for the mood disorders. Unlike in the anxiety disorders, however, there are sharp contrasts between the treatments for unipolar and bipolar disorders. There is even evidence that treatment of bipolar disorders as unipolar disorder (e.g., someone is treated for depression without realizing that they are having manic or mixed states as well), can trigger manic episodes and make symptoms worse. As such, proper diagnosis and cautious use of medications is crucial to effective treatment.

The prevalence of mood disorders is quite high in the general population, with 21.4% of the U.S. population meeting criteria for one of them across the lifespan. Unipolar disorders are much more common than bipolar ones (17% vs. 4.4% lifetime rates). In any given year, approximately 1 in 10 adults will qualify for a mood disorder diagnosis, with major impacts on the economy. Due to the high rate of functional impairment as well as high cost of health care, yearly costs of treatment alone for mood disorders is well over $10 billion. While that number is enormous, the total costs, including treatment of the disorder, treatment of other health care problems, and total lost work productivity, is a staggering $66 billion yearly. This number is even larger than the economic cost of the anxiety disorders, despite there being fewer persons who are diagnosed with mood disorders.

The remainder of this section of the book will be devoted to specific mood disorders. As with the anxiety disorders, for each mood disorder, the following information will be presented:

1) DSM-IV criteria (as reported in the DSM-IV-TR, published by the American Psychiatric Association in 2000)

2) Associated features (those things that are not part of the criteria, but are often seen in this population, commonly comorbid disorders, and impact of disorder on quality of life and functioning)

3) Child versus adult presentation (if and how the disorder presents different across the lifespan)

4) Gender and cultural differences (if and how the disorder varies between the sexes and around the world)

5) Epidemiology (the prevalence patterns of the disorder)

6) Etiology (what is known about the causes of the disorder)

7) Empirically supported treatments (those pharmacological and psychotherapeutic methods that have scientific evidence to back their use)

8) DSM-5 criteria revisions (when appropriate, there will be discussion of the reasons why the revisions are being proposed; full proposed diagnostic criteria can be viewed online at DSM5.org)

15

Key References

Druss, B.G., Marcus, S.C., Olfson, M., Tanielian, T., Elinson, L., & Pincus, H.A. (2001). Comparing the national economic burden of five chronic conditions. *Health Affairs, 20*(6), 233-241.

Fountoulakis, K. N. (2010). The emerging modern face of mood disorders: A didactic editorial with a detailed presentation of data and definitions. *Annals of General Psychiatry*, 9doi:10.1186/1744-859X-9-14

Kessler, R.C., Demler, O., Walters, E.E. (2005). Prevalence, severity, and comorbidity of twelve-month DSM-IV disorders in the National Comorbidity Survey Replication (NCS-R). *Archives of General Psychiatry, 62*, 617-627.

Rapaport, M., Clary, C., Fayyad, R., & Endicott, J. (2005). Quality-of-Life Impairment in Depressive and Anxiety Disorders. *The American Journal of Psychiatry, 162*(6), 1171-1178. doi:10.1176/appi.ajp.162.6.1171

Wang, P.S., Kessler, R.C. (2005). Global burden of mood disorders. In D. Stein, D. Kupfer, & A. Schatzberg (Eds.), *Textbook of Mood Disorders* (pp. 55-67). Washington DC: American Psychiatric Publishing, Inc.

Weissman, M.M., Bland, R.C., Canino, G.J., Faravelli, C., Greenwald, S., et al. (1996). Cross-national epidemiology of Major Depression and Bipolar Disorder. *JAMA, 276*(4), 293-299.

World Health Organization (2003). *The World Health Report 2003 - shaping the future*. Geneva, Switzerland.

Mood Disorder Episodes

In the DSM-IV, the mood disorders are differentiated by the patterns and types of episodes that a person experiences. As such, it is critical to have a solid knowledge of these episodes in order to fully understand the mood disorders. Below are descriptions of the different types of episodes seen in the mood disorders (e.g., major depressive, manic, hypomanic, and mixed), which are then followed by discussions of the possible specifiers placed on the mood disorders, and finally the disorders themselves (major depression, dysthymia, bipolar I and II, and cyclothymia). For the episodes, only DSM-IV criteria, associated features, and proposed DSM-5 changes to criteria will be addressed.

Major Depressive Episode (MDE)

DSM-IV-TR criteria

A. Five (or more) of the following symptoms have been present during the same 2-week period and represent a change from previous functioning; at least one of the symptoms is either (1) depressed mood or (2) loss of interest or pleasure. NOTE: Do not include symptoms that are clearly due to a general medical condition, or mood-incongruent delusions or hallucinations

1) Depressed mood most of the day, nearly every day, as indicated by either subjective report (e.g., feels sad or empty) or observation made by others (e.g., appears tearful). NOTE: In children and adolescents, can be irritable mood.

2) Markedly diminished interest or pleasure in all, or almost all, activities most of the day, nearly every day (as indicated by either subjective account or observation made by others)

3) Significant weight loss when not dieting or weight gain (e.g., a change of more than 5% of body weight in a month), or decrease or increase in appetite nearly every day. NOTE: In children, consider failure to make expected weight gains.

4) Insomnia or hypersomnia nearly every day

5) Psychomotor agitation or retardation nearly every day (observable by others, not merely subjective feelings of restlessness or being slowed down)

6) Fatigue or loss of energy nearly every day

7) Feelings of worthlessness or excessive or inappropriate guilt (which may be delusional) nearly every day (not merely self-reproach or guilt about being sick)

8) Diminished ability to think or concentrate, or indecisiveness, nearly every day (either by subjective account or as observed by others)

9) Recurrent thoughts of death (not just fear of dying), recurrent suicidal ideation without a specific plan, or a suicide attempt or a specific plan for committing suicide

B. The symptoms do not meet criteria for a Mixed Episode

C. The symptoms cause clinically significant distress or impairment in social, occupational, or other important areas of functioning.

D. The symptoms are not due to the direct physiological effects of a substance (e.g., a drug of abuse, a medication) or a general medical condition (e.g., hypothyroidism)

E. The symptoms are not better accounted for by bereavement, i.e., after the loss of a loved one; the symptoms persist for longer than 2 months or are characterized by marked functional impairment, morbid preoccupation with worthlessness suicidal ideation, psychotic symptoms, or psychomotor retardation.

Associated features

Individuals experiencing MDE often show irritability, general anxiety, phobias, worry over physical health, and complaints of pain. In addition, tearfulness, irritability, brooding, obsessive rumination can be seen. Panic attacks, although not common, can also seen during a MDE. These symptoms often cause problems with personal relationships, sexual functioning, and negatively impact the maintenance of relationships and marriages. Occupational and academic problems are not uncommon results of a MDE, as individuals may withdraw from or not complete responsibilities. Suicide risk is relatively high in individuals during a MDE, especially if they present with comorbid psychotic features. Sleep disruptions are seen in 40-60% of outpatients in a MDE, and in over 90% of inpatients.

Proposed DSM-5 Revisions

Few revisions are being proposed for MDE criteria. The changing of "symptoms" in criterion A to "criteria" is the first, with the dropping of "mood-incongruent delusions or hallucinations" from the same criterion the second. The last, largest proposed revision is that the exclusion for symptoms of bereavement be dropped, as there is no evidence to support that stressor being different from other types that could cause MDE symptoms.

19

Manic Episode (MNE)

DSM-IV-TR criteria

A. A distinct period of abnormally and persistently elevated, expansive, or irritable mood, lasting at least 1 week (or any duration if hospitalization is necessary).

B. During the period of mood disturbance, three (or more) of the following symptoms have persisted (four if the mood is only irritable) and have been present to a significant degree:

   1) inflated self-esteem or grandiosity
   2) decreased need for sleep (e.g., feels rested after only 3 hours of sleep)
   3) more talkative than usual or pressure to keep talking
   4) flight of ideas or subjective experience that thoughts are racing
   5) distractibility (i.e., attention too easily drawn to unimportant or irrelevant external stimuli)
   6) increase in goal-directed activity (either socially, at work or school, or sexually) or psychomotor agitation
   7) excessive involvement in pleasurable activities that have a high potential for painful consequences (e.g., engaging in unrestrained buying sprees, sexual indiscretions, or foolish business investments)

C. Mood disturbance is severe enough to cause marked impairment in occupational function, social activities, or relationships, or severe enough to necessitate hospitalization to prevent harm to self or to others.

D. At no time have delusions or hallucinations been present for two weeks in the absence of prominent mood symptoms.

E. The symptoms are not due to the direct physiological effects of a substance (e.g., a drug of abuse, a medication, or other treatment) or a general medical condition (e.g., hypothyroidism)

F. No organic factor is known that initiated or maintained the disturbance.

Associated features

In the midst of a MNE, many people a) do not realize that they are acting abnormally and b) resist attempts to get them treatment. They often become impulsive in decision making, which in turn often isolates people they are in close relationships with due to out of character behavior. Not infrequently, people in a MNE may display hypersexuality, both in terms of changing their physical appearance to be alluring and increasing sexual behaviors. Involvement in non-typical activities, such as money-making schemes, and displaying unethical behaviors may also occur. They may become hostile, threaten or physically assault others, or suicidal. When delusions and hallucinations are present, they are almost always mood-congruent (e.g., a person with elated mood may think or believe he has special powers).

Proposed DSM-5 Revisions

In contrast to major depressive episodes, a number of significant changes have been set forth for the description and criteria for manic episodes. First, recognition of markedly increased activity and energy as *the* core symptom of a MNE is built into the proposed criteria, along with the explanation that the symptoms should be present "most of the day, nearly every day" for at least one week. This brings the criteria in line with MDE wording and helps to clarify how present symptoms must be. Second, what was implicit before, that the change in energy and mood happen prior to Criterion B symptoms and that these symptoms are a distinct change from prior behaviors, is made explicit via improved wording. Some other, minor changes in wording are also being recommended (such as removing "pleasurable" from symptom 7).

Mixed Episode (MXE)

DSM-IV-TR criteria

A. The criteria are met both for a Manic Episode and for a Major Depressive Episode (except for duration) nearly every day during at least a 1-week period.

B. The mood disturbance is sufficiently severe to cause marked impairment in occupational functioning or in usual social activities or relationships with others, or there are psychotic features.

C. The symptoms are not due to the direct physiological effects of a substance (e.g., a drug of abuse, a medication, or other treatment) or a general medical condition (e.g., hyperthyroidism).

Associated features

Individuals experiencing a MXE may have disorganized thoughts or behavior and can sometimes appear to be psychotic, due to the presentation of depressive and manic symptoms simultaneously (e.g., crying uncontrollably but experiencing grandiose delusions). This combination may also increase risk of aggressive behaviors, both towards others and self-injurious acts. Substance use to harmful degrees are also quite common during a MXE, more so than during a MDE or MNE.

Proposed DSM-5 Revisions

Mixed episodes have been proposed for complete removal from the DSM-5, and will be replaced with the Mixed Features Specifier. It would apply to depressive, manic, and hypomanic episodes, with the rationale that it would help to describe someone's behavior more accurately than a mixed episode would. There has been disagreement and dissention in the literature over this change, with the primary concern being that someone presenting with depressive and manic symptoms would not meet criteria for bipolar disorder as a result of this specifier.

Hypomanic Episode (HME)

DSM-IV-TR criteria

A. A distinct period of persistently elevated, expansive, or irritable mood, lasting throughout at least 4 days, that is clearly different from the usual non-depressed mood. It is characterized as a period of increased energy that is not sufficient or severe enough to qualify as a Manic Episode.

B. During the period of mood disturbance, three (or more) of the following symptoms have persisted (four if the mood is only irritable) and have been present to a significant degree:

1) inflated self-esteem or grandiosity
2) decreased need for sleep (e.g., feels rested after only 3 hours of sleep)
3) more talkative than usual or pressure to keep talking
4) flight of ideas or subjective experience that thoughts are racing
5) distractibility (i.e., attention too easily drawn to unimportant or irrelevant external stimuli)
6) increase in goal-directed activity (either socially, at work or school, or sexually) or psychomotor agitation
7) excessive involvement in pleasurable activities that have a high potential for painful consequences (e.g., the person engages in unrestrained buying sprees, sexual indiscretions, or foolish business investments)

C. The episode is associated with an unequivocal change in functioning that is uncharacteristic of the person when not symptomatic

D. The disturbance in mood and the change in functioning are observable by others.

E. The episode is not severe enough to cause marked impairment in social or occupational functioning, or to necessitate hospitalization, and there are no psychotic features.

F. The symptoms are not due to the direct physiological effects of a substance (e.g., a drug of abuse, a medication, or other treatment) or a general medical condition (e.g., hyperthyroidism)

Associated features

HME episodes share many features with a MNE, but are less severe and tend to be less disruptive to a person's life. Clinically, HME can often be distinguished by a lack of psychotic features and grandiosity, as well as a coherence in thoughts and behaviors missing from people during a MNE. Hypersexuality is relatively common during a HME, and has been linked to increased creativity and productivity by some research. There are some researchers who support the idea that hypomania is not a pathological state, but instead evolutionarily beneficial and a stable personality trait, due to these features.

Proposed DSM-5 Revisions

As with the proposed changes to MNE, the DSM-5 is likely to increase the emphasis on increased activity and energy as the key symptom of hypomania. Also similar is the addition of the clarifying statement "most of the day, nearly every day" to assist in delineating how present symptoms should be, and making explicit that these behaviors represent a distinct change from the norm.

Mood Disorder Specifiers

As with many of the disorders in the DSM-IV, the mood disorders come with a host of specifiers, although not all are appropriate for every disorder (see below table). For those experiencing a MDE, coding specifies if one's symptoms are Mild, Moderate, Severe Without Psychotic Features, or Severe With Psychotic Features. Further, for those in a severe MDE and displaying psychotic features, one should also note if the features are mood congruent (consistent with depressive themes) or incongruent (non-depressive themes such as being persecuted, have people inserting thoughts into one's mind, and so on). Further, if some has met full criteria for a MDE, but does not do so now, they can be classified as being in Parital Remission (if some symptoms are present) or Full Remission (if no symptoms have been present during the last two months). For manic and mixed episodes, the exact same specifiers are used.

Major Depressive Disorder (MDD)

DSM-IV-TR criteria

There are two classifications of major depressive disorder in the DSM-IV: MDD, Single Episode and MDD, Recurrent. As might be expected, the only difference in criteria between the two is the number of major depressive episodes that one has experienced. It is important to note that for episodes to be considered separate and distinct, a two month minimum interval must come between them. In addition to the below criteria, the episode specifiers described previously would need to be used in order to fully describe the clinical status and features of the MDE.

A. Presence of a single Major Depressive Episode and a Unipolar disorder (MDD – Single Episode) OR Presence of two or more Major Depressive Episodes (MDD – Recurrent).

B. The Major Depressive Episode is not better accounted for by Schizoaffective Disorder and is not superimposed on Schizophrenia, Schizophreniform Disorder, Delusional Disorder, or Psychotic Disorder Not Otherwise Specified.

C. There has never been a Manic Episode, a Mixed Episode, or a Hypomanic Episode. NOTE: This exclusion does not apply if all of the manic-like, mixed-like, or hypomanic-like episodes are substance or treatment induced or are due to the direct physiological effects of a general medical condition.

If the full criteria are not currently met for a Major Depressive Episode, specify the current clinical status of the Major Depressive Disorder or features of the most recent episode:

In Partial Remission, In Full Remission
Chronic
With Catatonic Features
With Melancholic Features
With Atypical Features
With Postpartum Onset

Specify:

Longitudinal Course Specifiers (With and Without Interepisode
Recovery)
With Seasonal Pattern

Associated features

People with MDD experience a persistently low mood over several
days or weeks. As indicated above, other symptoms include loss of
interest in pleasurable activities (anhedonia), change in appetite, sleep
dysregulation, psychomotor retardation, a sense of worthlessness or
guilt, problems concentration, and thoughts of death or suicide.
MDD is highly comorbid with other disorders, particularly those on
the anxiety spectrum. In adults and adolescents, research shows
clinical samples have comorbidity rates between 40-70%. In
epidemiological samples as many as 75% of depressed youth have
been observed to suffer from an anxiety disorder, as do over 59% of
adults. Substance use is a common co-occurrence as well (24%),
although those diagnosed with substance dependence show rates of
MDD over twice as high as those with only substance abuse.
Interestingly, about 30% of individuals with MDD also meet criteria
for an impulse control disorder, such as intermittent explosive
disorder, pathological gambling, conduct disorder, oppositional
defiant disorder, or antisocial personality disorder.

28

MDD can be devastating to one's life, with almost 97% of those meeting diagnostic criteria reporting at least some role impairment. A substantial body of literature has examined the decreases in quality of life and functioning that occur for those experiencing a MDE and even between episodes. Indeed, one study found that QoL is worse for those with MDD than in all of the anxiety disorders, with the exception of PTSD. In patients with MDD, around 60% report severe impairment from their disease on QoL, and that even after improvements in symptoms these impairments persist. Job functioning is the most well-studied area, with studies showing those with MDD perform worse at work than persons with rheumatoid arthritis, and are five times as likely to become unemployed. This same relationship has been found with other chronically physically ill populations. There are also negative impacts from MDD on physical health, lowering immunological functioning, thereby increasing risk of catching communicable diseases. Presence of MDD also increases risk of developing other diseases, such as Type II diabetes, cardiovascular disease, and chronic pain. Another major area of study is the impact of maternal depression on children, with findings indicating MDD in mothers is highly predictive of a number of poor outcomes in children (e.g., increased risk of psychological problems, lowered academic performance).

Suicide and suicidal ideation are common in the MDD population. Studies have found that up to 75% of those who successfully commit suicide suffer from a mood disorder of some kind. While reported rates of completed suicide in people with MDD range as high as 15%, better controlled, population based studies have found much lower rates (7% for males, 1% for females). Depression alone, however, is not the whole story. Interestingly, while presence of depression is a major risk factor for suicidal ideation, it is not predictive of actual suicidal behavior. Instead, presence of severe anxiety and disorders characterized by poor impulse control (such as substance abuse or borderline personality disorder) when combined with depression is a major risk factor. For example, one study found that over 40% of completed suicides had comorbid depressive and substance use disorders. Men are more likely to successfully complete suicide than women, and older males even more so. This is primarily due to men using more lethal methods (shooting themselves, hanging, car crashes) than women (more likely to cut their wrists or overdose on medications). While attempts are most common between the ages of 25-44, completed suicides are the most frequent in those age 65 or older.

Child vs. adult presentation

While the symptoms of MDD are the same in children and adults, the characteristics of the disorder does change across the lifespan. For instance, prior to puberty, there are no differences in prevalence rates in males and females, but starting in adolescence females begin to outnumber males by a 2:1 ratio. In terms of symptoms, children with MDD are more likely to exhibit irritability and social withdrawal than adults. Separation anxiety is frequent in children, and somatic complaints are more common as well. Melancholic symptoms, delusions, and suicide attempts are seen less frequently in children. With the move into adolescence and adulthood, symptoms of psychomotor retardation and sleep disturbance become more common. In geriatric populations, MDD is often accompanied by disorientation, memory loss, and distractibility.

Gender and cultural differences in presentation

One of the most replicated, cross-cultural findings in the study of MDD has been the gender differences in prevalence rates. Females are much more likely to qualify for a diagnosis than males, both for one-year rates (8.6% vs. 4.9%) and across the lifespan (20.2% vs. 13.2%). Interestingly, these gender differences in rate are usually not seen prior to adolescence, but with the onset of puberty (12-14 years old) become very noticeable. While symptom severity and functional impairment are similar across genders, several studies have found slight differences in symptom presentation for both adolescents and adults. Females, for instance, report higher rates of appetite increase, sleep difficulties, and weight gain than males. Self-reported distress, anxiety, and somatic complaints are also more common in females. In the realm of functional impairment, males reported that MDD caused a higher interference in work functioning, while females report greater levels of marital problems. In terms of disease course, a body of longitudinal research has shown that females are more likely to experience chronic, recurrent depression.

While all ethnicities and cultures have been found to experience MDD, there are major differences in antidepressant use in depressed minority populations compared to depressed Caucasians in the U.S., (9-17% vs. 41%, respectively). This is likely indicative of poorer access to and acceptance of mental health treatment among minorities, as treatment effectiveness for medications is similar across all ethnic groups, rather than differences in prevalence. Comparing Western to Eastern cultures, however, results in vastly differing prevalence rates, with those in Western cultures over three times as likely to experience MDD at some point. Cross-national studies have found widely varying rates, with several finding slightly higher rates of depression in more well-developed, richer countries than poorer, developing ones (14.6% vs. 11.1%).

Culture can influence symptoms of depression, both in terms of experience and how these problems are communicated to health professionals. Several theorists have attempted to explain these differences, with many pointing to cultural differences in positivity, views of the self and role in society, and presentation of distress. Clinically, under or misdiagnosis can be reduced by being alert to differing presenting depressive complaints across ethnicity and cultures. For example, in some cultures, depression may be experienced largely in somatic terms, rather than with the sadness or guilt so common in Western countries. For example, Hispanics, Latinos and people from Mediterranean cultures report headaches and nerve problems more frequently, while Asian cultures tend to

31

describe more feelings of weakness, tiredness, or imbalance. Those from Middle Eastern cultures may complain about problems of the heart, while some Native American tribes, such as the Hopi, discuss depression in terms of "heartbreak."

Epidemiology

MDD is among the most commonly diagnosed mental disorders worldwide. In the United States, 16.9% of the population will experience at least one episode of MDD during their lifetime, with 12-month prevalence rates a much lower 6.8%. In children, rates of MDD are approximately 2%, increasing to between 4-8% during adolescence. Age and cohort effects are present, with a larger proportion of people under 60 qualifying for a diagnosis at some point (16.0-20.1%) than those above 60 (10.7%). A similar pattern of more frequent MDD is also present during one-year prevalence studies (7.0-8.4% under 60, 2.9% over 60). Cross-nationally, rates are generally lower than seen in the U.S., with higher rates for Western countries (e.g., Canada at 11.4% and New Zealand at 16.3% for lifetime prevalence) than non-Western ones (e.g., Puerto Rico at 5.5 and South Korea at 4.1%).

Etiology

Like all mental disorders, the genesis of depression comes not from only one source, but instead from biological, psychological, and social factors. First, MDD appears to be highly influenced by genetic and biological factors. Studies on identical twins reared in the same environment show they have about a 40% chance of both developing depression, while fraternal twins raised in the same environment only have about a 20% chance of both developing depression. Adoption studies support a genetic influence, finding that children of depressed mothers are more susceptible to depression even when raised in home environments with no depression present. Exactly how genetics contributes to depression, though, is the cause of much study and debate.

Biologically, a number of factors have been found to differ between depressed and non-depressed individuals, with most today stressing the role of gene-environment interaction and the subsequent role of numerous biological systems. There are not, though, many strong conclusions about depression and biology, despite thousands of studies and decades of research on the issue. While abnormal neurotransmission is a repeated finding, with serotonin, norepiniphrine, dopamine, GABA, and acetylcholine all found to be dysregulated in one way or another, it is unclear that this is the cause of depressive symptoms. Instead, these dysregulations may stem from other brain dysfunctions in the brain or from environmental stressors. For example, much research has focused on the role that chronic stressors can have on the HPA axis, part of the neuroendocrine system that controls reactions to stress and regulates digestion, immunological functioning, mood and emotion regulation, sexuality, and energy storage and expenditure, among others. A dysfunctional HPA axis could then result in numerous cascading problems in the body and brain, including alterations in neurotransmitter release and absorption, hippocampal neurogensis defects, and problems in how the brain processes environment rewards. These changes would then cause problems in neurotransmitter function, as well as a loss of neuroplasticity in the brain, which in turn would be responsible for the maintenance of depression, as the brain loses its ability to change and adapt when faced with new stimuli and information. These in turn cause a lowering of prefrontal activity, as well as possible decreases in a number of brain areas, including the hippocampus, amygdala, and others.

Many environmental factors can influence depression, with one overall finding being that stressful life events can greatly contribute to development. Although everyone experiences stressors in their life, those predisposed to or experiencing depression report stressors occurring more frequently (at rates 2.5 times the general population) and being able to cope with them less effectively. Many depressogenic events are losses, such as the death of a family member, losing a long-standing job, getting divorced, and so on. Other major environmental risk factors include traumatic experiences as a child, low socioeconomic status, few close friends, and having a serious illness. While these are often seen as triggers for depressive episodes, the maintaining factors appear to be more related to biological factors (as discussed above) and psychological factors (below).

While numerous psychological theories of depression have been put forth over the past 100 years, only those that have had the most impact on development of effective treatments will be reviewed here. The earliest psychological model that resulted in an empirical decline in depressive symptoms was Aaron Beck's cognitive model. Beck proposed that negative early life experiences resulted in automatic negative thought patterns, commonly called cognitive distortions or dysfunctional beliefs, that in turn result in maladaptive interpretations of internal and external stimuli. These distortions cause a depressed person to view their self, the world, and the future (the negative cognitive triad) in a very pessimistic fashion. In other words, it is as if the person is seeing the world through "depression-colored glasses," concentrating and focusing on negative events or stimuli, interpreting ambiguous things as negative, and ignoring or discounting positive events. From this Beck developed his cognitive therapy for depression, which focused on challenging and changing the way depressed people interpret their environmental stimuli.

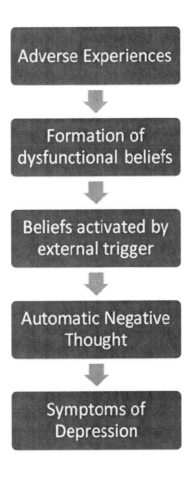

Both Albert Bandura's social learning and Martin Seligman's learned helpless models further expanded this psychological theory, helping to explain how events external to the individual can help both cause and maintain these negative outlooks, while Peter Lewinsohn's work on the lack of positive reinforcement in a depressed individual's environment also contributed to a growing understanding of psychological factors at play. The eventual integration of these cognitive, learning, and behavioral explanations helped to guide the creation of one the most effective treatments for depression, cognitive-behavioral therapy (described below).

Interpersonal models of depression developed by Gerald Klerman were based on the work of Harry Stack Sullivan. Klerman emphasized that depression occurs in the context of an individual's social relationships, regardless of possible origins in biology or genetics. Two primary assumptions underlie this model: 1) Current interpersonal problems have their roots in early dysfunctional relationships; and 2) Current interpersonal problems are likely to be involved in precipitating/perpetuating current symptoms. As depression causes an impact on relationships with others, this causes a negative cycle to develop. To wit, the more depressed we become, the more our relationships are impaired, which in turn makes us more depressed, which makes our relations even more impaired, and so on.

Empirically supported treatments

Compared to the anxiety disorders, where a limited range of pharmacological agents and cognitive-behavioral therapy are the only treatments with strong support for their use, there are a wider variety of evidence-based treatments available for those experiencing major depressive symptoms. Pharmacologically, the primary medications are very similar to those used in the anxiety disorders (SSRIs and SNRIs). In terms of direct brain interventions, electroconvulsive therapy (ECT) is well studied, while transcrainal magnetic stimulation (TCM) and vagus nerve stimulation are both still building a solid evidence base. Therapeutically, cognitive, behavioral, and interpersonal therapies (IPT) all have a large amount of support for their usage across the lifespan. It is worth noting that there is some emerging support for the use of exercise to treat chronic MDD, as well as the use of light therapy for seasonally determined MDD, also known as seasonal affective disorder.

Treatment guidelines generally recommend that, for those with mild depressive symptoms, mild impairment and no history of prior depressions, treatment should consist of psychoeducation, support, and case management. Even with this "placebo" type of treatment, the majority of those who are mildly depressed will experience symptom alleviation and relief. This is unsurprising, given that recent meta-analyses have shown that placebo drug treatment, while it shows lower effect sizes than active drug treatments, can account for up to 67% of the improvement in drug trials (effects sizes of 1.69 vs. 2.50). For moderate depressive symptoms and impairment, monotherapy (either medications or psychotherapy) are recommended, dictated by patient preference and availability of properly trained providers. Finally, for those who do not respond to monotherapy and those with severe symptoms and impairment, a combination of medications and CBT or IPT is indicated. For those who are prescribed antidepressant medications, physician monitoring is critical due to the high non-adherence or discontinuing rates. Studies have shown that about a third of persons prescribed antidepressants discontinue within a month of beginning their treatment, and 40% stop taking the medications by three months. While the emergence of side effects certainly contributes to this, other factors, such as lack of response and social stigma, can also contribute.

Pharmacologically, the first line treatments of choice are collectively referred to as the second-generation antidepressants (ADs). These are primarily SSRIs (such as fluoxetine, fluvoxamine, sertraline, and citalopram) or SNRIs (such as venlafaxine or duloxetine), although there are some other agents that influence serotonin and noradrenalin in this category. Although dosages between second generation antidepressants varies greatly, treatment outcome studies comparing efficacy across medications has shown few indications that any is clearly superior to the others. There are also no clear predictors of who will respond most positively to what medication; there is consensus that if a medication has worked well for patient's family member with MDD, that is a solid starting point. Tricyclic antidepressants (TCA) and monoamine oxidase inhibitors (MAOI) are older medications that have as strong of treatment effects as newer medications, but are considered second- and third-line medications due to tolerability and safety concerns (e.g., higher rates of side effects), need for dietary restrictions, and potential interactions with other common medications.

ADs are associated with a number of significant side effects. The most commonly reported side effects are sexual in nature, including decreased libido, erectile problems, and difficulty achieving orgasm or ejaculation. Other common side effects are gastrointestinal problems (e.g., nausea, diarrhea), mild sedation, dizziness, and dry mouth. One major concern is often the "black-box warning" included on newer antidepressants that warns of the possibility for "emergent suicidality" when taking these medications. This warning was primarily the result of public outcry over several highly publicized incidents of completed suicide in children shortly after they began taking SSRIs. While it is true that in children and adolescents there is evidence for up to a two-fold increase in suicidal thoughts and behaviors, it is important to note that in the very large clinical trial literature there were no actual completed suicides. The research literature is very clear, though, that there is no support for first-line ADs causing emergent suicidal thoughts or behaviors in adults across the lifespan.

In terms of psychotherapy, two broad classes of treatment have been repeatedly empirically supported for reducing MDD symptoms and are considered first-line treatments: cognitive-behavioral and interpersonal therapy. Effect sizes for CBT compared to placebos and wait-list control groups are around 1.0, similar to medication wait-list controls. Patients doing CBT have a lower dropout rate than is seen in most medication trials, people doing "maintenance" CBT (e.g., being seen approximately once a month after the initial 12-15 sessions) show relapse rates similar to those who are using medication on an ongoing basis. The basic premise behind CBT for MDD is based on the research and work by Beck and Lewinsohn in the late 1960s and 1970s. Beck's early work focused on cognitive models of depression, emphasizing the role of our thoughts about and interpretations of events in the development and maintenance of depression. Lewinsohn, in contrast, focused on how a low rate of positive reinforcement in the environment caused people to withdraw from social interactions and engaging in potentially reinforcing behaviors, resulting in depression. While the cognitive model became more widely accepted, it incorporated a number of behavioral components into it, morphing from CT to CBT. Research spearheaded by Neil Jacobson in the late 1990s, though, was able to show that only the behavioral portion of CBT, called behavioral activation (BA), was at least as effective as CT alone, as well as the full treatment package of CBT. Interestingly, one study found that BA was superior to CBT in the treatment of severe depression. Regardless, CT, BA, and CBT are all well supported for immediate and long-term MDD treatment. Below, I will describe CBT, rather than CT and BA alone, but readings in the reference sections delver further into each.

Much like for generalized anxiety disorder, CBT for MDD focuses on assisting patients in identifying cognitions (thoughts, images, or ideas) that are both automatic (quickly pop into one's mind, not deliberate) and negative in tone, usually about themselves, the world, and the future, collectively known as the negative cognitive triad.. Then, patients are taught to challenge such thoughts with reason, logic, and evidence. This is done based on the theory that people with depression have dysfunctional beliefs that, when activated, cause the behavioral, cognitive, affective, and somatic symptoms of depression. For example, a person experiencing depression may hold the belief that they are an incompetent, unlikeable individual, that the entire world views them as such, and that there will not be any chance for this to change in the future. The behavioral portion of treatment focuses on putting these beliefs to the test, particularly through scheduling actions designed to increase positive outcomes, rather than just withdrawing from and avoiding activities. These activations are not just scheduling of pleasant events (e.g., going out to eat ice cream), but instead focus on helping someone escape problematic coping patterns. For example, someone may schedule a specific time to do their laundry, because doing so will increase their feeling of mastery over events (e.g., "I did this laundry instead of just feeling bad because I had put it off for so long. Now I'm not ruminating over how much I haven't done around the house."). These behavioral and cognitive changes in turn result in changes of a person's dysfunctional beliefs, alleviating depressive symptoms.

Interpersonal therapy was also developed in the late 1960s and 1970s and focuses on one's current interpersonal relationships and the surrounding social context, in contrast to the self-focus of CBT. IPT grows from the belief that, regardless of the root biopsychosocial cause of depression, it occurs within the context of interpersonal relationships. In other words, depression negatively impacts how we interact with others, which in turn makes us further depressed. Four areas of potential problems are discussed in IPT: grief after loss, conflict in currently significant relationships, adapting to change, and social isolation. The therapist them assists the patient in skill-building exercises designed to improve interpersonal functioning and increase social support. Key changes a client makes are being able to link mood changes to relationship events, communicate feelings and/or expectations appropriately, and use problem solving when confronted with relationship difficulties. Typical treatment length for IPT ranges between 6-20 sessions depending on severity of problems and comorbidity issues, and maintenance treatment is recommended as necessary.

Research support is strong for IPT relieving depression in adolescents and adults, although not in younger populations. Large scale studies comparing IPT to placebo pills show greater response in IPT, and equal response to medications alone. A combination of IPT and medications, however, does not appear to increase response rate. Comparisons of IPT and CBT show that they are generally equivalent in effect sizes, drop-out rate, and long-term outcome. It should be noted, however, that there are some questions about these findings, as blind raters often have a hard time differentiating the two treatments and that when IPT is closer to "ideal" CBT, it is more effective.

As mentioned before, a number of other treatments have received support for use in treating MDD. In terms of first-line evidence and recommendations, though, they primarily are restricted to special populations and not general use. For example, in terms of neurostimulation, electroconvulsive therapy (ECT) is considered a treatment of choice *if* someone has been treatment resistant to psychotherapy and medications, they are acutely suicidal, or are having MDD with psychotic features. Repetitive transcranial magnetic stimulation (rTMS) is another neurostimulation technique that is showing promise, but has less definitive evidence and lower remission rates that therapy or medications. Light therapy, which involves daily exposure to very bright light (typically around 30,000 lux) for about a half hour a day, has been well-supported for the treatment of season MDD, sometimes referred to as seasonal affective disorder. Taking St. John's Wort, which has an unknown mechanism of action, has been found to be superior to placebo and produce effects for those with mild to moderate depression, but not severe depressive symptoms. The research base for other therapies, such as exercise and taking Omega-3 fatty acid supplements, is growing but not yet large enough to support their use routinely over other therapies discussed above.

Proposed DSM-5 Revisions

There are almost no changes being proposed to the MDD criteria, and those that are deal exclusively with the specifiers. The removal of "Severe" in the "With Psychotic Features" specifer is proposed to separate the severity rating from the subtype, as MDD with psychotic features is not always severe. The other changes deal with having "mood-congruent" and "mood-incongruent" specifiers and extending the length of time for postpartum onset to 6 months after giving birth.

Key References

Ablon, J.S., & Jones, E.F. (2002). Validity of controlled clinical trials of psychotherapy: Findings from the NIMH Treatment of Depression Collaborative Research Program. *American Journal of Psychiatry, 159*, 775-783.

Bennett, D.S., Ambrosini, P.J., Kudes, D., Metz, C., & Rabinovich, H. (2005). Gender differences in adolescent depression: Do symptoms differ for boys and girls? *Journal of Affective Disorders, 89*, 35-44.

Bernert, S., Matschinger, H., Alonso, J., Haro, J.M., et al. (2009). Is it always the same? Variability of depressive symptoms across six European countries. *Psychiatry Research, 168*, 137-144.

Bromet, E., Andrade, L., Hwang, I., Sampson, N., Alonso, J., de Girolamo, G., & ... Kessler, R. (2011). Cross-national epidemiology of DSM-IV major depressive episode. *BMC Medicine*, 990.

Fountoulakis, K.N. (2010). The emerging face of mood disorders. *Annals of General Psychiatry, 9* (14). Available from http://www.annals-general-psychiatry.com/content/9/1/14

Kennedy, S.H., Lam, R.W., Parikh, S.V., Patten, S.B., & Ravindran, A.V. (2009). Canadian Network for Mood and Anxiety Treatments (CANMAT) Clinical guidelines for the management of major depressive disorder in adults. *Journal of Affective Disorders, 117*, S1–S2.

Kessler, R.C., Berglund, P., Demler, O., Jin, R., Kortez, R., et al. (2003). The epidemiology of Major Depressive Disorder: Results from National Comorbidity Survey – Replication (NCS-R). *JAMA, 289*, 3095-3105.

Krishnan, V., & Nestler, E.J. (2008). The molecular neurobiology of depression. *Nature, 455*(16), 894-902.

Kornstein, S.G., Schatzburg, A.F., Thase, M.A., Yonkers, K.D., McCullough, J.P. et al. (2000). Gender differences in chronic major and double depression. *Journal of Affective Disorders, 60,* 1-11.

Nock, M.K., Hwang, I., Sampson, N.A., & Kessler, R.C. (2010). Mental disorders, comorbidity, and suicidal behavior: Results from the National Comorbidity Survey Replication. *Molecular Psychiatry, 15,* 868-876.

Richards, D. (2011). Prevalence and clinical course of depression: A review. *Clinical Psychology Review, 31,* 1117-1125.

Rief, W., Nestroiuc, Y., Weiss, S., Welzel, E., Barsky, A.J., & Hofmann, S.G. (2009). Meta-analysis of the placebo response in antidepressant trials. *Journal of Affective Disorders, 118,* 1-8.

Trinh, N-H., T., Shyu, I., McGrath, P.J., Clain, A., Baer, L., et al. (2011). Examining the role of race and ethnicity in relapse rates of major depressive disorder. *Comprehensive Psychiatry, 52,* 151-155.

Dysthymic Disorder (DD)

DSM-IV-TR criteria

A. Depressed mood for most of the day, for more days than not, as indicated either by subjective account or observation by others, for at least 2 years. NOTE: In children and adolescents, mood can be irritable and duration must be at least 1 year. The individual must have been depressed for at least 22 months during the past 2 years. This type of disorder is classified as unipolar, where there is only severe depression.

B. Presence, while depressed, of two (or more) of the following:

  1) poor appetite or overeating
  2) insomnia or hypersomnia
  3) low energy or fatigue
  4) low self-esteem
  5) poor concentration or difficulty making decisions
  6) feelings of hopelessness

C. During the 2-year period (1 year for children or adolescents) of the disturbance, the person has never been without the symptoms in Criteria A and B for more than 2 months at a time.

D. No Major Depressive Episode has been present during the first 2 years of the disturbance (1 year for children and adolescents); i.e., the disturbance is not better accounted for by chronic Major Depressive Disorder, or Major Depressive Disorder, In Partial Remission.

E. NOTE: There may have been a previous Major Depressive Episode provided there was a full remission (no significant signs or symptoms for 2 months) before development of the Dysthymic Disorder, there may be superimposed episodes of Major Depressive Disorder, in which case both diagnoses may be given when the criteria are met for a Major Depressive Disorder

F. There has never been a Manic Episode, a Mixed Episode, or a Hypomanic Episode, and criteria have never been met for Cyclothymic Disorder.

G. The disturbance does not occur exclusively during the course of a chronic Psychotic Disorder, such as Schizophrenia or Delusional Disorder.

H. The symptoms are not due to the direct physiological effects of a substance (e.g., a drug of abuse, a medication) or a general medical condition (e.g., hypothyroidism).

I. The symptoms cause clinically significant distress or impairment in social, occupational, or other important areas of functioning.

Dysthymia specifiers include Early Onset (before age 21 years), Late Onset (age 21 years or older), and With Atypical Features.

Associated features

Given that DD is often conceptualized as a low grade, chronic depressive state, it should not be surprising that there are significant overlaps between it and MDD. Some of the most common symptoms seen in those with DD are feelings of inadequacy, social withdrawal, a general loss of interest in once enjoyed activities, feelings of guilt or brooding about the past, irritability and excessive anger, and decreased activity and productivity. Compared to MDD, though, certain symptoms are seen less often. These include changes in sleep patterns and appetite, significant weight gain or loss, and psychomotor symptoms. Developing DD also puts you at an increased risk for experiencing a major depressive episode, as around 75 percent of adults with DD will qualify for a diagnosis of MDD at some point in the next five years. Research looking at risk for such a "double depression" in youth, though, has been highly inconsistent, with studies finding rates anywhere between 17-70%. Spontaneous remission of DD is much lower than in MDD, with remission rates as low as 10% and as high as 30% over a 10 year period.

Impairment from DD appears to differ somewhat from that seen in MDD. Although there is less symptom severity at any one time point, DD is more impairing overall due to it's longitudinal nature. For example, in youth major impairments in peer relationships and functioning are apparent, consequently placing one at high risk for a number of impairments in school, home, and social functioning. Experiencing DD as a child or adolescent also appears to disrupt later, adult functioning to a greater degree than MDD does, most likely because of the lower amount of symptom-free periods during critical developmental periods. Longitudinal studies comparing those with DD and MDD have found much higher rates of inpatient hospitalizations and suicide attempts and completions in dythymic adults than those experiencing major depression. In addition, higher rates of anxiety, personality, and substance use disorders are found among the DD population. Higher rates of disability and lower rates of ability to work full time are seen in DD compared to MDD, with related higher self-reports of work impairment due to emotional problems. One study comparing adults with DD to adults with schizophrenia found lower quality of life in the DD population among the areas of physical health and leisure activities, pointing to the very negative impact dysthymia has on functioning.

Comorbidity is extremely common in DD, with over 75% of adults having at least one comorbid disorder. The most commonly seen comorbids include major depressive disorder, the anxiety disorders (particularly generalized anxiety and social anxiety), and substance use problems (with alcohol abuse or dependence being the most common). In children, approximately half qualify for another diagnosis, with the most commonly co-occurring problems are generalized anxiety, simple phobias, and externalizing disorders such as ADHD and oppositional defiant disorder. Some 15% of youth will have more than one cormorbid disorder.

Child vs. adult presentation

One of the major differences in DD presentation among children is length. The DSM-IV-TR requires only one year of symptom expression in youth, compared to two years needed in adults. Much like in MDD, many children present with greater symptoms of irritability than adults, although adolescents tend to present with both irritability and depressed mood. In children, DD occurs at equal rates across both sexes, but shows a much higher prevalence of females (approximately a 2:1 ratio) by middle adolescence. Research has shown that certain DD symptoms, such as lack of appetite, feeling fatigued, and excessive sleeping, are almost nonexistent in youth, while disruptive behavior and disobedience are much more prevalent than in adults.

Gender and cultural differences in presentation

The ratio of males to females in DD changes significantly from childhood to adulthood. While rates appear to be roughly equal for prepubertal children, with the onset of adolescence the ratios begin to shift. By middle adolescence, there are almost twice as many females as males who are diagnosed with DD, a trend that continues into adulthood. In adults, one year prevalence rates are around 1.9%

in females and 1.0% in males, while lifetime rates are approximately 3.1% in females and 1.8% in males.

Little research has examined cross-cultural differences in DD, with that which has being unequivocal in their findings. One major study that examined prevalence rates in the U.S. found significantly lower rates of DD in Hispanics (2.2%) and blacks (3.5%) than in whites (4.3%), while another study looking at Chinese-Americans found higher lifetime rates (5.2%). Interestingly, equal number of males and females in the Chinese-American population experienced dysthymia, a major difference from research on other ethnic groups in the U.S. A second large scale study comparing African-Americans, Mexican-Americans, and whites found higher rates for the minority groups (7.5% and 7.4%, respectively) than whites (5.7%). Much more research on these issues needs to be undertaken.

Epidemiology

Dysthymia is much less common than MDD in studies looking at both one year (1.5% vs. 6.8%) and lifetime (2.5% vs. 16.9%) prevalence rates. Interestingly, though, it is one of the most commonly seen diagnoses in mental health clinics, with between 22-36% of people in outpatient settings qualifying for this diagnosis. A different pattern of age effects are seen in DD compared to MDD, with rates gradually increasing from the 18-29 (1.8%) to 30-44 (2.8%) to 45-59 (3.8%), then dropping back down for the over 60 group (1.3%). Rates for youth with DD have varied greatly across studies, ranging anywhere from 0.6-4.6% in children and 1.6-8.0% in teens.

Etiology

Compared to MDD and bipolar disorder, the etiological causes of dysthymia have been much less well researched. As mentioned previously, DD is often considered to a lower-grade, but more chronic version, of MDD, and as such most hypotheses regarding etiology are similar to those concerning the causes of major depression. Unfortunately, given the small number of studies, the primary importance of environmental or biological factors is not established. There are certainly biological and genetic factors partially responsible, as DD shows strong familial relationships. Having a parent or other close relative with either MDD or DD greatly increases the risk of someone developing dysthymia. There have not been many well-controlled studies examining neurobiological aspects of DD, but some aspects that have been found include serotonin disruption, sleep disruptions, and MAO dysfunction.

Environmental factors such as a negative home environment with high amounts of isolation and low amounts of social support and non-depressive parental psychopathology, particularly personality disorders, have been linked to DD development in youth. The small amounts of research looking at risk factors in adolescents have found that being physically abused can trigger DD onset, as can the severe illness or death of an immediate family member. As can be told based on the brevity of this section, though, much more research needs to occur to truly understand the causes of dysthymia.

Empirically supported treatments

As with so many other things, treatment for DD is an adaptation of treatments for MDD. Both psychological and pharmacological treatments have been studied, and several recent meta-analyses have greatly increased our understanding of what does and does not work. A recent study which pooled the results of over 1450 patients with DD in treatment outcome studies found that antidepressants (primarily SSRIs) worked significantly better than placebos, with response rates of 52.4% vs. 29.9%. Interestingly, patients with DD show a lower treatment response to placebos than those with MDD, even though the antidepressant response rates were not statistically different. Response to SSRIs has been found to be better than that to TCAs, but no differences between type of SSRI used were discovered.

Psychotherapy meta-analyses have shown a small but significant effect compared to control groups (effect size of 0.23), although it is a much smaller effect than that seen for psychological treatments for MDD. Although there are not many head-to-head studies comparing different types of psychotherapy to each other, those that do have found no difference between CBT, IPT, and brief supportive therapy effectiveness. Studies that have examined both pharmacological and psychological treatment, however, have shown that medications are significantly more effective than therapy alone, and that the combined usage of medication and therapy are superior to either alone (effect size of 0.42).

Proposed DSM-5 Revisions

The first major proposed change is to rename DD "Chronic Depressive Disorder." Essentially, this indicates a collapsing together of dysthymia and major depressive disorder with a chronic specifier. This is occurring due to numerous studies over the past 15 years which indicate no reliable or valid differences between these groups on family history, demographics, symptoms, or treatment response. As such, the other major change is the removal of the DSM-IV criteria D, which excluded persons with major depressive episodes.

Key References

Cuijpers, P., van Staten, A., Schuurmans, J., van Oppen, P., Hollon, S.D., & Andersson, G. (2010). Psychotherapy for chronic major depression and dysthymia: A meta-analysis. *Clinical Psychology Review,* *30*(1), 51-62

Gureje, O. (2011). Dysthymia in a cross-cultural perspective. *Current Opinion in Psychiatry,* 24(1), 67-71.

Hellerstein, D. J., Agosti, V., Bosi, M., & Black, S. R. (2010). Impairment in psychosocial functioning associated with dysthymic disorder in the NESARC study. *Journal of Affective Disorders, 127*(1-3), 84-88.

Klein, D.N., Shankman, S.A., & Rose, S. (2006). Ten year prospective follow-up study of the naturalistic course of dysthymic disorder and double depression. *American Journal of Psychiatry, 163* ,872-880.

Kornstein, S.G., Schatzberg, A.F., Thase, M.E., Yonkers, K.A., McCullough, J.P., et al. (2000). Gender differences in chronic major and double depression. *Journal of Affective Disorders, 60,* 1-11.

Levkovitz, Y., Tedeschini, E., & Papakostas, G.I. (2011). Efficacy of antidepressants for dysthymia: A meta-analysis of placebo-controlled randomized trials. *Journal of Clinical Psychiatry, 72*(4), 509-514.

Lizardi, H., & Klein, D.N. (2000). Parental psychopathology and reports of the childhood home environment in adults with early-onset dysthymic disorder. *Journal of Nervous Mental Disorders, 188,* 63–70.

Nobile, M., Cataldo, G., Marino, C., & Molteni, M. (2003). Diagnosis and treatment of dysthymia in children and adolescents. *CNS Drugs, 17*(13), 927-46

Rheburg, D., Beekman, A.T.F., de Graaf, R., Nolen, W.A., Spijker, J., et al. (2009). The three-year naturalistic course of dysthymic disorder and double depression. *Journal of Affective Disorders, 115,* 450-459.

Bipolar Disorder

In the DSM-IV-TR, a distinction is made between two types of Bipolar Disorder (see full critiera below). In bipolar I, patients have manic episodes with or without depressive episodes, while in bipolar II they have hypomanic and depressive episodes. For the purposes of this section, both will be discussed concurrently, with any specific differences between areas below (e.g., functional impact, epidemiology) highlighted.

DSM-IV-TR criteria

(Please note that there are six separate sets of criteria for bipolar I, which specify the nature of the most recent episode, but only one set for bipolar II. Specifiers differ slightly for each as well.)

Bipolar I Disorder, Single Manic Episode

A. Presence of only one Manic Episode and no past major Depressive Episodes.

B. The Manic Episode is not better accounted for by Schizoaffective Disorder and is not superimposed on Schizophrenia, Schizophreniform Disorder, Delusional Disorder, or Psychotic Disorder Not Otherwise Specified.

Specify if Mixed (criteria met for a Mixed Episode), severity level (mild, moderate, severe without psychotic features or severe with psychotic features), with catatonic features or postpartum onset, and current clinical status (in partial or full remission).

Bipolar I Disorder, Most Recent Episode Hypomanic

A. Currently (or most recently) in a Hypomanic Episode

B. There has previously been at least one Manic Episode or Mixed Episode

C. The mood symptoms cause clinically significant distress or impairment in social, occupational, or other important areas of functioning.

D. The mood episodes in Criteria a and B are not better accounted for by Schizoaffective Disorder and are not superimposed on Schizophrenia, Schizophreniform Disorder, Delusional Disorder, or Psychotic Disorder Not Otherwise Specified.

Specify the longitudinal Course (with or without interepisode recovery), if with seasonal pattern of depressive episodes, or with rapid cycling.

Bipolar I Disorder, Most Recent Episode Manic

A. Currently (or most recently) in a Manic Episode

B. There has previously been at least one Major Depressive Episode, Manic Episode, or Mixed Episode

C. The mood episodes in Criteria A and B are not better accounted for by Schizoaffective Disorder and are not superimposed on Schizophrenia, Schizophreniform Disorder, Delusional Disorder, or Psychotic Disorder Not Otherwise Specified.

Specify the longitudinal Course (with or without interepisode recovery), if with seasonal pattern of depressive episodes, or with rapid cycling.

Bipolar I Disorder, Most Recent Episode Mixed

    A. Currently (or most recently) in a Mixed Episode

    B. There has previously been at least one Major Depressive episode, Manic Episode, or Mixed Episode

    C. The mood episodes in Criteria A and B are not better accounted for by Schizoaffective Disorder and are not superimposed on Schizophrenia, Schizophreniform Disorder, Delusional Disorder, or Psychotic Disorder Not Otherwise Specified.

Specify severity level (mild, moderate, severe without psychotic features or severe with psychotic features), with catatonic features or postpartum onset, current clinical status (in partial or full remission), longitudinal Course (with or without interepisode recovery), if with seasonal pattern of depressive episodes, or with rapid cycling.

Bipolar I Disorder, most Recent Episode Depressed

    A. Currently (or most recently) in a Major Depressive Episode

    B. There has previously been at least one Manic Episode or Mixed Episode

    C. The mood episodes in Criteria A and B are not better accounted for by Schizoaffective Disorder and are not superimposed on Schizophrenia, Schizophreniform

Disorder, Delusional Disorder, or Psychotic Disorder Not Otherwise Specified.

Specify severity level (mild, moderate, severe without psychotic features or severe with psychotic features), chronic, with catatonic features or postpartum onset, with melancholic or atypical features, current clinical status (in partial or full remission), longitudinal Course (with or without interepisode recovery), if with seasonal pattern of depressive episodes, or with rapid cycling.

Bipolar II Disorder

A. Presence (or history) of one or more Major Depressive Episodes.

B. Presence (or history) of at least one Hypomanic Episode.

C. There has never been a Manic Episode or a Mixed Episode.

D. The mood symptoms in Criteria A and B are not better accounted for by Schizoaffective Disorder and are not superimposed on Schizophrenia, Schizophreniform Disorder, Delusional Disorder, or Psychotic Disorder Not Otherwise Specified.

E. The symptoms cause clinically significant distress or impairment in social, occupational, or other important areas of functioning.

Specify current/most recent episode type, severity level (mild, moderate, severe without psychotic features or severe with psychotic features), chronic, with catatonic features or postpartum onset, with melancholic or atypical features, current clinical status (in partial or full remission), longitudinal Course (with or without interepisode recovery), if with seasonal pattern of depressive episodes, or with rapid cycling.

Associated features

Aside from the diagnostic criteria, many other problems are associated with the presence of bipolar disorder. Impulsivity is a prominent component of manic and hypomanic episodes, and is associated with impulsivity and its consequences, including increased risk of substance abuse and violent or suicidal behavior. Violent behaviors could include child abuse, spouse abuse, or other worse violent actions. Problems with school such as truancy or failure are common in adolescents and young adults, and later in life occupational success is also very difficult to attain or maintain. Maintaining stable relationships is also a problem for individuals with bipolar disorder, and divorce is common. These social and occupational problems persist even during asymptomatic periods, as persons with bipolar disorder show overall lower quality of life than controls even during symptom-free periods. Depending on the study, only a third or so of people with bipolar disorder achieve functional recovery, despite being asymptomatic. Direct comparisons between bipolar and unipolar depression have found decreased general health, social functioning, and emotional health in bipolar populations. These functioning decreases and the resultant costs to society in terms of treatment and lost productivity are estimated to cost the U.S. over $50 billion per year.

Specific cognitive impairments have been found across the bipolar disorders, but to varying degrees. Research has found that, compared to controls, performance levels in verbal memory, working memory, psychomotor speed, and executive function were reduced in bipolar I disorder patients, but that performance levels in only working memory and psychomotor speed were reduced in bipolar II disorder patients. Bipolar I patients have also been found to be impaired across cognitive domains (except for visual memory), while bipolar

59

II patients were unimpaired on verbal memory measures. Two factors that could be involved in bipolar I patients having more severe neuropsychological deficits are the presence of psychotic symptoms and the effect of medication. Bipolar I patients generally have a history of more frequent psychotic symptoms, and as such antipsychotic treatments are used more frequently in patients with Bipolar I. Some studies have associated cognitive deficits with antipsychotic medication rather than with psychotic symptoms; however, the effect of medication is difficult to control for and to evaluate in a clinical setting.

Comorbidity is rampant in the bipolar population, with 60-85% of patients qualifying for two or more Axis I disorders. Epidemiological and clinical data have found that 45-75% of persons diagnosed with bipolar disorder qualify for an anxiety disorder, with GAD and panic disorder being the most common. Individuals with bipolar disorders are also prone to substance abuse (21-34%), with nicotine the highest used drug, followed by alcohol. For illegal substances, marijuana has the highest abuse rate. Borderline personality disorder is also commonly co-diagnosed, with rates of 20-30%.

Suicide attempts and completions are very prevalent in individuals with bipolar disorders, making it among the most deadly of mental disorders. It is estimated that between 10-15% of this group will complete suicide. Suicidal behavior is most often related to the depressive aspects of the disease, as the highest levels of suicide ideation were at the point when individuals had mixed phases of the illness and then peaking off into the more depressive stages. As such, suicidal ideation and attempts are more likely to occur in Bipolar Disorder II rather than Bipolar Disorder I because bipolar II patients spend more time during the mixed phases of depression. Interestingly, there is a much lower attempt to completion ratio in patients with bipolar disorder than in other disorders, with a 3:1 attempt to completion ratio in this population, compared to a national average of approximately 30:1. Prediction of suicide attempts appears to rely most heavily on comorbid substance abuse, but completions are seen more often in those with comorbid anxiety disorders.

There is a fairly substantial amount of literature that has examined the link between bipolar disorders and creativity. Many musicians, writers, artists, and other highly creative people have been either retrospectively or currently diagnosed with bipolar disorders, including Pete Wentz of the band Fall Out Boy, Linda Hamilton of the *Terminator* films, comedian Russell Brand, Carrie Fisher of *Star Wars* fame, and notable historical figures such as Jackson Pollock, Vincent van Gogh, and Virginia Woolf. Controlled studies have found higher rates of bipolar disorders in contemporary writers compared to normal controls, higher levels of objective creativity in adults with bipolar disorder compared to controls, and higher levels of creativity in children whose parents have been diagnosed with bipolar disorder.

Child vs. adult presentation

In youth, diagnosis of a bipolar disorder is a uniquely American phenomenon, and a relatively new one at that. It's has only been over the last decade that many children or adolescents have been given a bipolar diagnosis, and there is enormous controversy over this. For example, rates of diagnosis in outpatient clinics doubled over the past 15 years to 6%, with the number of office visits for children and adolescents with bipolar disorder in the United States increasing 40-fold from 20,000 in 1994–95 to 800,000 in 2002–03. Given the lack of corresponding increases outside of the U.S. in similar counties, for example in the United Kingdom and Germany, many have criticized this increase. Particularly troubling is the fact that many of those top researchers and clinicians promoting the diagnosis and subsequent pharmacological treatment of children have direct financial ties to the pharmaceutical industry in the form of speaking and consulting fees. Many have raised the concern that, with so many direct financial ties to the industry, it is highly unlikely that these researchers are conducting bias-free research. Then there is the fact that the two primary groups conducting pediatric bipolar research (Geller and colleagues at Washington University and Biederman and colleagues at Harvard) have very different conceptualizations of bipolar disorder in children. Biderman's recent exposure as having collected close to $2 million in fees from companies whose drugs he was investigating, as well as communications from him promising that positive results would be found for their medications, just solidified that there is an immense amount of reason to be suspect of these increases in diagnosis.

Given all these caveats, exactly what can we say about bipolar disorder in youth? First, that there is very strong evidence for the presence of a "classic" bipolar presentation in youth. A number of converging lines of research all point to this fact, meaning that any other definition of a bipolar disorder or subtype in children must be measured against this standard. That being said, at the present time there are some established differences in adolescent and adult bipolar disorder. For example, mixed episodes occur more often in adolescents and young adults and appear to decrease in frequency as one ages. Manic episodes in adolescents are more likely to include psychotic features and may be associated with school truancy, antisocial behavior, school failure, or substance abuse. A significant minority of adolescents appear to have a history of long-standing behavior problems that precede the onset of an outright manic episode, but it is unclear if these problems represent a prolonged prodromal period to expression of bipolar disorder or an independent disorder. Between 10-15% of adolescents with recurrent major depressive episodes will develop bipolar I disorder by early adulthood.

Gender and cultural differences in presentation

In stark contrast to the unipolar mood disorders (and most anxiety disorders), there are not discernible gender differences in bipolar I rates. Interestingly, though, there do seem to be slightly higher number of females that qualify for bipolar II disorders, likely due to the gender differences in depressive symptoms. In addition, rapid cycling (having four or more mood episodes during a 12 month period) and depression with psychotic features are more common in women. Gender does appear to impact the course of the disorder, as males are more likely to have manic episodes first, while women are most likely to first manifest major depressive episodes. This initial difference seems to carry on throughout the course of the disorder, as males tend to have more manic episodes and fewer depressive episodes across the lifetime. Other noted gender differences include comorbidity, as males are more often diagnosed with substance use disorders, while women have a higher prevalence rate of personality disorders. Females also have higher rates of attempted suicide, although the males' attempts are much more violent in nature (as seen in unipolar depression as well).

There has not been a reported difference in race or ethnicity and the presence of bipolar I or II. Rather, cultural differences appear to impact the presentation and course of the disorder, not the prevalence. For example, the course of bipolar disorder may be worse among African-American patients, who are more likely to have attempted suicide and been hospitalized compared to Caucasians. Further, African-American adolescents with bipolar disorder are treated for longer periods with atypical antipsychotics than Caucasian adolescents, even after adjusting for the severity of psychotic symptoms. Research comparing those in the U.S. and China have found several significant differences, including higher substance abuse and depressive symptoms as well as longer periods of mania in the American population.

Epidemiology

Taken as a whole, the bipolar spectrum disorders (bipolar I, bipolar II, cyclothymia) have a one year prevalence rate of approximately 2.8%, with a slightly higher lifetime prevalence of 4.4%. Specifically, bipolar I and II have very similar lifetime rates, at 1.0% and 1.1%, respectively. Depending on the type of measurement used, between 2-5% of the population display sub-clinical levels of bipolar symptoms (meeting some but not all of the criteria). Bipolar disorders are much more prevalent in younger age groups and decline in frequency with age. For example, one year rates fall from a high of 4.7% in 18-29 year olds to only 0.7% of those over age 60.

Etiology

Biological and genetic factors play a large role in the development of bipolar disorder. First degree biological relatives of those with bipolar disorder have a higher chance of developing it themselves compared to the general public, with studies showing rates of 4-24% (compared with 1% in the normal population). Twin studies show bipolar I concordance rates of 40-85% for identical twins and 10-20% for dizygotic pairs, further evidence of genetic influence. Bipolar II, though, shows lower heritability rates overall. This points to the distinct nature of these disorders, as does linkage and association studies showing that there is no single "bipolar" gene, but instead many genes that appear to influence development in conjunction with other biological and environmental factors. In particular, genes that help to regulate the production of serotonin, dopamine, and glutamate have all been implicated in and associated with bipolar disorder. Biologically, studies have identified several areas of brain functioning that are abnormal in people diagnosed with bipolar disorder. Differences in the prefrontal cortex, anterior cingulate cortex, hippocampus, and amygdala have all been found compared to control subjects, although given the small sample sizes and differing methodologies, broad statements concerning these are hard to make.

Psychosocial factors have been implicated in both onset of bipolar disorder and risk of relapse. Some research indicates that intense stressors, primarily interpersonal ones, can be causally linked to initial mood episodes (depressive or manic), but that subsequent ones are increasingly less influenced by stress. Early childhood trauma and abuse are frequent in this population, and may help to trigger an earlier onset of symptoms and higher rates of comorbidity with the anxiety disorders. The most comprehensive theories of bipolar disorder, though, are those that integrate psychological, social, and biological influences to help explain the emergence of bipolar disorder. At present, two biopsychosocial models of bipolar disorder are emerging: the behavioral approach system (BAS) dysregulation theory and the circadian and social rhythm theory.

Key to the BAS dysregulation theory is the idea that there are two primary psychobiological systems present in humans that regulate behavior: the behavioral approach system and the behavioral inhibition system (BIS). While the BIS is responsible for inhibition of behavior, most often in response to possible punishment or threat through initiation of locomotor activity, the BAS is responsible for motivation and reward drives. Biologically, it has been posited that this involves the dopaminergic system and several areas of the prefrontal cortex, such as the anterior cingulate and the orbitofrontal cortices. In many individuals with bipolar disorder, the BAS appears to be hypersensitive to potential activators, such as events that involve attaining or striving for goals or events that stymie goal attainment and cause anger. For those with hypersensitive BAS, these events cause an excessive level of activation, which in turn puts one at an elevated risk for manic or hypomanic symptoms. In the event that one experiences failure in achieving goals, though, BAS deactivation appears to occur, which would then put one at an elevated risk for depressive symptoms. Research has supported this theory in terms of both depressive and manic episodes, and one study even showed that persons diagnosed with bipolar disorder that purposefully decreased goal-directed activity in the beginning stages of hypomania, thus not activating the BAS, had fewer subsequent manic episodes. This theory also helps to explain the decreased amount of stress needed to activate episodes across life, as the BAS become increasingly sensitive to stimuli, although longitudinal studies examining this are absent as of yet. Importantly, this model uses a relatively parsimonious explanation for a highly diverse set of symptoms and presentations by focusing on a single diathesis – the dysregulation of the BAS – that responds differentially to specific environmental stimuli and triggers.

The second comprehensive model of bipolar disorder is referred to variously as the social zeitgebers theory (zeitgebers being German for "time-givers") or social rhythm disruption (SRD) theory. The key idea behind this theory is that certain environmental cues, including meal times, scheduled exercise, alarm clocks, or the regular presence of certain individuals, serve to imbed certain rhythms in us socially, which work in conjunction with our natural or circadian rhythms and processes. Disruption to those zeitgebers then causes a disruption of our social and, subsequently, biological rhythms. These disruptions then play a causal role in triggering mood episodes, manic and depressive. While several studies have supported the fact that many on the bipolar spectrum have irregular social rhythms, from both self-report and behavioral assessment, research has been mixed regarding a causal link between disruptions and mood episode onset.

Empirically supported treatments

In distinct contrast to most of the disorders presented in this book, first line treatments for bipolar disorder are pharmacological, not psychological, even for lower-level symptoms (e.g., bipolar II versus bipolar I). Psychotherapy is seen primarily as an adjunctive treatment, albeit a useful one. The first effective medication for bipolar disorder, and one still frequently prescribed and considered the gold standard of treatment, is lithium carbonate. Additionally, studies over the last 20 years have found a total of 11 drugs effective for management of acute bipolar mania. While these are primarily dopamine antagonists (such as olanzapine, haloperidol, and aripiprazole), there are three non-dopamingeric agents (lithium, valproate, and carbamazepine) with support. Direct comparisons between these agents have not found differential treatment effects, but studies have shown that olanzapine and aripiprazole are more tolerable for patients than divalproex and haloperidol, respectively. The management of bipolar depression has traditionally received less attention than mania, although a flurry of research in the past 10 years has attempted to address this issue. Current evidence points to the use of one of two treatments as first-line for depression in the context of bipolar disorder: quetiapine and the combination of olazepine and fluoxetine. Antidepressant medication is *not* recommended for those experiencing a bipolar depression, as a small number of people may have a manic episode triggered by these medications. For those persons with bipolar disorder who are not actively experiencing a mood episode, studies have shown that relapse prevention can be obtained via several medications recognized as first line options, including the aforementioned drugs of lithium, olanzapine, and quetiapine. Further, evidence is clear in pointing out that an abrupt discontinuation of medication places one at very high risk for lapsing back into a manic or depressive state.

A small amount of research has examined the use of physical treatments for bipolar disorder, primarily electroconvulsive therapy (ECT) and other brain stimulation techniques. Although very small in number, there is some promise to the use of these treatments, either adjunctively or as standalone options. For example, one study found that ECT plus chlorpromazine compared to a sham ECT plus chlorpromazine was able to treat acutely manic patients faster and with a higher rate of recovery. Older studies showed high rates of response to ECT in medication non-responders as well (56-69%). These studies, however, were for the most part comparing ECT to newer pharmacological agents and lacked adequate placebo arms (e.g., a sham form of ECT). As such, ECT is generally considered a

67

second-line treatment for mania or if someone is a medication non-responder. Research examining the use of ECT in bipolar depression is promising, with some indications that it may be more effective than in unipolar depression. Still, though, the research base is relatively small at this point, and as such it is most often considered a second or third line treatment. A primary reason for this is that some patients receiving ECT may experience a switch from a depressive to manic state, and that the risk for this appears to be higher in bipolar depression. Other brain stimulation techniques, such as repetitive Transcranial Magnetic Stimulation (rTMS), are currently being investigated but do not have a solid evidence base in place.

The two psychological treatments that have been most well researched as adjunctive therapies are cognitive-behavior therapy (CBT) and interpersonal and social rhythm therapy (IPSRT). Both have shown significant decreases in relapses, need for medication, hospitalization rates, and increases in overall functioning and adherence to medication. Unfortunately, as in the anxiety disorders, there is a paucity of well-trained psychologists and therapists in these modalities, which hampers access. There is strong evidence that psychoeducation alone is useful for reducing relapse rates as well. This typically involves information about symptoms, course of the disorder, treatment options, early warning signs of relapse into mood episodes, and potential triggers of episodes. Both CBT and IPSRT have a strong element of education in them as well, which may very well be the "active" ingredient in those treatments. In addition, CBT also focuses on identifying dysfunctional and maladaptive thoughts then correcting them via cognitive restructuring. IPSRT focuses on helping patients achieve a steady social rhythm and address interpersonal concerns and problems that have arisen due to a person's disorder. Again, it should be stressed that these are adjunctive treatments, not first line options.

Proposed DSM-5 Revisions

The most controversial change proposed for the DSM-V surrounds the case of pediatric bipolar disorder. Although there are not specific criteria proposed for that diagnosis, a separate diagnosis termed "temper dysregulation disorder with dysphoria" was developed by the Mood Disorders Workgroup, creating a category for youth with symptoms of mood instability. Despite acknowledging some of the limitations and concerns with such a diagnosis, particularly that the research supporting it has only been conducted by a single researcher's group, the Workgroup nonetheless felt that this would be a worthy diagnosis in that it calls attention to a group of children that are most likely currently being diagnosed as having pediatric bipolar disorder, despite not showing the "classic" bipolar I or II symptoms. Interestingly, longitudinal research on these children, though, shows them more likely to be diagnosed with depression in later life, not bipolar disorder. As such, many researchers and clinicians have strong reservations about this new diagnostic category and see it as more of a "stopgap" measure rather than a well-constructed disorder.

Key References

Birmaher, B., Axelson, D., Monk, K., Kalas, C., Goldstein, B., et al. (2009). Lifetime psychiatric disorders in school-aged offspring of parents with bipolar disorder: the Pittsburgh Bipolar Offspring study. *Archives of General Psychiatry, 66*(3), 287-296.

da Costa, R.T., Rangé, B.P., Malagris, L.E., Sardinha, A., de Carvalho, M.R., & Nardi, A.E. (2010). Cognitive-behavioral therapy for bipolar disorder. *Expert Review of Neurotherapuetics, 10,* 1089–1099.

Galvez, J.F., Thommi, S., & Ghaemi, S.N. (2011). Positive aspects of mental illness: A review in bipolar disorder. *Journal of Affective Disorders, 128* (3), 185-190.

Grandin, L. D., Alloy, L. B., & Abramson, L. Y. (2006). The social zeitgeber theory, circadian rhythms, and mood disorders: Review and evaluation. *Clinical Psychology Review, 26*(6), 679–694.

Hirschowitz, J., Kolevzon, A., & Garakani, A. (2010). The pharmacological treatment of bipolar disorder: The question of modern advances. *Harvard Review of Psychiatry, 18*(5), 266-278.

Loo, C., Katalinic, N., Mitchell, P.B., & Greenberg, B. (2011). Physical treatments for bipolar disorder: A review of electroconvulsive therapy, stereotactic surgery and other brain stimulation techniques. *Journal of Affective Disorders, 132*, 1-13.

Mantere, O., Isometsa, E., Ketokivi, M., Kiviruusu, O., Suominen, K., et al. (2010). A prospective latent analysis of psychiatric comorbidity in DSM-IV bipolar I and II disorders. *Bipolar Disorders, 12*, 271-284.

Michalak, E. E., Murray, G., Young, A. H., & Lam, R. W. (2008). Burden of bipolar depression: Impact of disorder and medications on quality of life. *CNS Drugs, 22*(5), 389-406.

Nivoli, A.M.A., Colom, F., Murru, A., Pacchiarotti, I., Castro-Loli, P., et al. (2011). New treatment guidelines for acute bipolar depression: A systematic review. *Journal of Affective Disorders, 129*, 14-26.

Nivoli, A.M.A., Pacchiarotti, I., Rosa, A.R., Popovic, D., Murru, A., et al. (2011). Gender differences in a cohort study of 604 bipolar patients: The role of predominant polarity. *Journal of Affective Disorders, 133*, 443-449.

Olfman, S. (2007). *Bipolar Children: Cutting-Edge Controversy, Insights, and Research.* Praeger: Santa Barbara, CA.

Robbins, B.D., Higgins, M., Fisher, M., & Over, K. (2011). Conflicts of interest in research on antipsychotic treatment of pediatric bipolar disorder, temper dysregulation disorder, and attenuated psychotic symptoms syndrome: Exploring the unholy alliance between Big Pharma and psychiatry. *Journal of Psychological Issues in Organizational Culture, 1*(4), 32-49.

Simon, G.E.,, Hunkeler, E., Fireman, B., Lee, J.Y., & Savarino, J. (2007). Risk of suicide attempt and suicide death in patients treated for bipolar disorder. *Bipolar Disorders, 9* (5), 526-530.

Strakowski, S. M., Shang-Ying, T., DelBello, M. P., Chiao-Chicy, C., Fleck, D. E., Adler, C. M., & ... Amicone, J. (2007). Outcome following a first manic episode: Cross-national US and Taiwan comparison. *Bipolar Disorders, 9*(8), 820-827.

Urošević, S., Abramson, L.Y., Harmon-Jones, E., & Alloy, L.B. (2008). Dysregulation of the behavioral approach system (BAS) in bipolar spectrum disorders: Review of theory and evidence. *Clinical Psychology Review, 28,* 1188–1205

Yatham, L.N., Kennedy, S.H., O'Donovan, C., et al. (2005). Canadian Network for Mood and Anxiety Treatments (CANMAT) guidelines for the management of patients with bipolar disorder: consensus and controversies. *Bipolar Disorders, 7* (suppl. 3), 5–69.

Cyclothymic Disorder

DSM-IV-TR criteria

A. For at least 2 years, the presence of numerous periods with hypomanic symptoms and numerous periods with depressive symptoms that do not meet criteria for a Major Depressive Episode. (in children and adolescents, the duration must be at least 1 year).

B. During the above 2 year period (1 year in children and adolescents), the person has not been without the symptoms in Criteria A for more than 2 months at a time

C. No Major Depressive Episode, Manic Episode, or Mixed Episode has been present during the first 2 years of the disturbance.

D. Note: After the initial 2 years (1 year in children and adolescents) of Cyclothymic Disorder, there may be superimposed Manic or Mixed Episodes (in which case both Bipolar 1 Disorder and Cyclothymic Disorder may be diagnosed) or Major Depressive Episode (in which case both Bipolar 2 Disorder and Cyclothymic Disorder may be diagnosed).

E. The symptoms in Criteria A are not better accounted for by Schizoaffective Disorder and are not superimposed on Schizophrenia, Schizophreniform Disorder, Delusional Disorder, or Psychotic Disorder Not Otherwise Specified.

F. The symptoms are not due to the direct physiological effects of a substance (e.g. a drug abuse, a medication) or a general medical conditioned (e.g. hyperthyroidism).

G. The symptoms cause clinically significant distress or impairment in social, occupational, or other important areas of functioning.

Associated features

Compared to bipolar I or II disorder, research is relatively sparse on cyclothymic disorder, or cyclothymia. Although part of the bipolar spectrum disorders, it is considered a less severe but still chronic problem, both in terms of symptoms and functional impact. The individual experiences numerous hypomanic episodes and many periods of depression over a two year period. It is important to note, though, that these depressive periods do not meet criteria for a major depressive episode. Mood disturbances can last days to weeks, with periods of normal moods lasting up to one month. Much more so than other disorders discussed in this book, cyclothymia treads the line between a mental disorder and normal fluctuations in mood and behavior, and in fact most people who qualify for this diagnosis based on symptoms alone do not seek treatment or experience functional impairment.

This is not to say that some individuals do not have impairment or disruptions to their life, though, as the symptoms can impact relationships in both social and familial realms. Depressive symptoms, for example, may cause loss of productivity at work, while hypomanic symptoms may cause difficulty in romantic relationships via impulsive behaviors without thought of their consequence. This leads to very intense, but often short, romances and relationships. The lack of predictability of mood shifts is often reported to be particularly frustrating for both patients and their families. Approximately 50% of those diagnosed with cyclothymia have a comorbid substance abuse disorder, most commonly alcohol or stimulants. While shifts from cyclothymia to bipolar I are rare, there have been studies showing anywhere from a 15 to 50 percent risk for moving up to a bipolar II diagnosis. As in bipolar I and II, many patients with this diagnosis display higher levels of creativity and artistic temperament than in control populations.

Child vs. adult presentation

Diagnostically, children and adolescents only need symptoms to be present for one year to qualify for this disorder (as opposed to two years in adults). There is some evidence to suggest that the presence of cyclothymia is more impairing in children than adults, as it can cause a larger disruption to social relationships and disturb the development of emotional regulation. Symptom presentation, however, appears to be similar across ages.

Gender and cultural differences in presentation

Cyclothymia seems to be equally common in men and women, although women are more likely to present for treatment in clinical settings. No research has studied the potential impact of culture or ethnicity on cyclothymia presentation, although it is generally thought that, like in bipolar disorder, there would be little influence.

Epidemiology

Lifetime prevalence rates have ranged from 0.4% to 1% in the U.S. In specialty outpatient mood disorder clinics, between 3-5% of persons meet diagnostic criteria.

Etiology

The genetic and biological underpinning of cyclothymia is reinforced through studies that show mood disorders, including Major Depressive Disorder and Bipolar I or II, are more common in first-degree biological relatives of people with cyclothymia. Also, cyclothymia is seen more often in relatives of those with bipolar I than the normal population. Psychosocially, it has been posited that disruption of social rhythms could be casually linked to changes from normal to hypomanic or depressive moods, although no research has examined this.

Empirically supported treatments

Similar to how treatments for dysthymia were downward extensions and adaptations of treatments for major depression, treatments for cyclothymia have been extended from bipolar disorder. But, as before, there is a lack of scientific literature in this area. Low dosages of those medications used to treat bipolar disorder, such as lithium or valproate, are commonly given and appear to have both stabilizing properties and prevent reoccurrence of hypomanic or depressive symptoms. Psychotherapy has not been well-studied, but education on symptoms and possible triggers for mood fluctuation have been emphasized in the literature, as well as guidance on tailoring their lifestyle to be more tolerant of mood swings (such as working a job where they can set the hours). Similar education could also be provided to family members, in order that they could be more understanding, if not accepting, of the varying behavior of the individual. In what was the first randomized clinical trial of any type of psychotherapy for cyclothymia by Fava and colleagues, they reported on a cognitive-behavioral intervention modeled on those developed for bipolar disorder that consisted of ten sessions across 5 months. They found both immediate and longitudinal differences in depressive and hypomanic symptoms as far as two years post treatment compared to a supportive, nondirective control group.

Proposed DSM-V Revisions

No changes have been proposed for cyclothymia in the next edition of the DSM.

Key References

Akiskal, H.S. (2001). Dysthymia and cyclothymia in psychiatric practice a century after Kraepelin. *Journal of Affective Disorders, 62*, 17-31.

Bisol, L.W., & Lara, D.R. (2001). Low-dose quetiapine for patients with dysregulation of hyperthymic and cyclothymic temperaments. *Journal of Psychopharmacology, 24*, 421–424.

Fava, G.A., Rafanelli, C., Tomba, E., Guidi, J., & Grandi, S. (2011). The sequential combination of cognitive behavioral treatment and well-being therapy in cyclothymic disorder. *Psychotherapy and Psychosomatics, 80*, 136-143.

Jacobsen, F.M. (1993). Low-dose valproate: a new treatment for cyclothymia, mild rapid-cycling disorders and premenstrual syndrome. *Journal of Clinical Psychiatry, 54*, 229–234.

Shen, G.H., Sylvia, L.G., Allloy, L.B., Barrett, F., Kohner, M., et al. (2008). Lifestyle regularity and cyclothyic symptomatology. *Journal of Clinical Psychology, 64*, 482–500.

Vázquez, G.H., Kahn, V., Schiavo, C.E., Goldchluk, A., Herbst, L., et al. (2008). Bipolar disorders and affective temperaments: national family study testing the 'endophenotype' and 'subaffective' theses using the TEMPS-A Buenos Aires. *Journal of Affective Disorders, 108,* 25-32.

Other Mood Disorders

In addition the disorders reviewed above, there are four others included in the DSM-IV mood disorder section. The first is *Mood Disorder Due to a General Medical Condition*. As expected from the name, this is where a person experience depressive or mania problems as a direct result of a medical problem, including degenerative neurological conditions such as Parkinson's or Huntington's disease, cerebrovascular, metabolic conditions, autoimmune conditions, endocrine conditions, or cancer. The second is *Substance-Induced Mood Disorder*, which is the direct result of either intoxication or withdrawal from a psychoactive substance. Mood symptoms can occur as a result of intoxication from alcohol, amphetamines, cocaine, hallucinogens, inhalants, opioids, phencyclidine, sedatives, hypnotics, and anxiolytics. Withdraw from these can also cause mood dysfunction. The final ones are *Depressive Disorder Not Otherwise Specified* and *Bipolar Disorder Not Otherwise Specified*. These are "catch-all" category, where a person displays prominent mood dysregulation symptoms, but does not meet full criteria for any of the other, specific disorders.

Finally, there are two disorders being recommended for inclusion in the DSM-V that are new to that edition. First is a diagnostic category of *Mixed Anxiety-Depression*. The proposed criteria include three or four symptoms of major depression combined with two or more symptoms of anxiety. This is a category that was proposed for inclusion into the DSM-IV, and further research has supported it as a common problem. The other proposed disorder is *Premenstrual Dysphoric Disorder*, wherein a large number of depressive symptoms are experienced regularly prior to onset of menstruation, and then resolve themselves postmenses. As with all other disorders, a key feature of both would be the associated distress and dysfunction as a result of the symptoms.

CPSIA information can be obtained at www.ICGtesting.com
Printed in the USA
BVOW04s2145110913

330974BV00007B/66/P